The Real Nature
Of Mystical Experience

VINCIT
OMNIA
VERITAS

The Real Nature
of
Mystical Experience

By
Gopi Krishna

Bethel Publishers, Inc. • Darien, Connecticut 06820

Gopi Krishna

Published by Bethel Publishers, Inc.
P. O. 1134, Darien, CT 06820
Library of Congress Cataloging-in-Publication Data
The Real Nature of Mystical Experience
ISBN 978-0-941136-143
This edition is printed on acid-free paper that meets the
American National Standards Institute Z39.48 Standard.

1. Spirituality.
4. Evolution Studies. 5. Human Potential. 6. Anthropology.
7. Psychology. I. Title.

CONTENTS

CHAPTER 1

Mystical Experience
The Target of Human Evolution

The ideas expressed and the conclusions drawn in this work about the real nature of mystical experience are offered in a spirit of utter humility with an open mind and a sense of preparedness to revise them if, after more than forty years' day and night critical observation of my own extraordinary mental state, I am still proved to be wrong.

These opinions and conclusions, if correct, are of the utmost importance for the race; so important that, from my point of view, there is no other topic of such urgency and importance at this time. The urgency lies in the fact that, from what is revealed to me, the human brain is still in a state of biological evolution and that the tempo of this evolution has become so fast that a rethinking on and a readjustment of the current values as also the whole social and political fabric of mankind has become necessary.

Constant tensions and pressures in the world situation, a general sense of discontent and lack of peace, a foreboding of approaching disaster, widespread use of drugs, the revolt of youth, tragedies of marital life and a pressing urge in countless minds to rise above reality by religious striving, Yoga, meditation, esoteric disciplines or occult practices pro-

1

vide convincing evidence for what I say. It is palpably clear that the general mental climate of the earth is not the same as it was at the beginning of the Second World War or even in 1950. But we do not know what factors have combined to cause this rapid change. Why is the gap between older and rising generations all over the earth becoming noticeably larger and more difficult to reconcile?

What mystical experience has to do with the environment of the earth will soon become apparent. The class of human beings that has exerted the greatest influence on the thinking and behavior of mankind has been that of the prophets, saviors and mystics, including the founders of all current faiths. Kings, philosophers, rulers, scientists or scholars have, all combined, and played a secondary role. Revealed religious teaching has held a fascination and maintained a grip on the human mind that is unmatched in any other sphere of life. This grip has persisted for thousands of years. Why?

What makes millions upon millions of human beings believe implicitly in the words of the founder of their faith even in this rational age? While literally flooded by the marvels of technology, why do the masses still have greater faith in the ideals of their religion and the teachings of prophets or saints than in the rational expositions of scientists and philosophers alike? Why do even distinguished scientists subscribe to faith? What is the explanation for this paradox?

There are examples where even those rationalists who were rank atheists in youth turned religious towards the close of life. Even materialistic political ideologies have not been able to uproot this inherent urge in the masses. No psychologist or thinker has so far provided a rational explanation for this apparently erratic behavior of the human mind. I am suggesting for the first time an explanation for the profound phenomenon of religion for close examination and empirical verification by the learned of our day. I do so with a full sense of my responsibility and the duty I owe to mankind and to God.

From my point of view, religious experience is not to be treated lightly and cannot form a subject on which everyone can write or talk. It is of the profoundest significance and importance to mankind. This is the reason why deepest secrecy has always been maintained in respect of the esoteric doctrines of faith and why the hidden truths about God and soul were talked of with bated breath. It has always been felt instinctively that religion is a sacred subject beyond the province of the intellect.

In India, the massive *Vedas* were committed to memory and transmitted orally, generation after generation, for centuries—a prodigious feat—because there was a subconscious awareness that what they contained was of the utmost importance for mankind. The concern shown by theologians for every word and line of the gospels of all faiths to preserve them from distortion or interpolation has also been due to the same intuitive impulse.

The reason is that mystical vision or, in other words, the vision of God, is the target of human evolution. Those who had it in the right form exerted a tremendous fascination on the mind of others as they were the first arrivals at a destination for which all of us are bound. Their teachings have been cherished and acted upon with the utmost care, because they contain hints and guidelines about the Path which all of us have to traverse to reach the same stage.

The interpretation that the first Founders of various faiths were special envoys deputed by the Creator is, from my point of view, only partially true, based more on personal convictions than on truth. This interpretation has tended to restrict the benefit these great souls came to confer on all mankind, for it created a climate of rivalry and even animosity between the adherents of different faiths, each determined to allot the place of precedence to its own founder.

Since there are millions upon millions of devoted followers in each faith, no one can decide whose claim is true. The outcome has been that the founder of one faith does not hold the same position of honor in the other. The upshot is that instead of commanding universal homage, as the first recipients of Grace, which lifted them up to a lofty spiritual height to which all human beings have to climb, they became objects of adoration only to one segment of humanity and of indifference, antipathy and even hate to the others.

This has created an anomalous position which cannot be overlooked any longer. Harmony between religions and unanimity among the followers of various faiths are of utmost importance to plug every possible loophole for dispute and discord among human beings.

What political wrangles can arise and what scenes of bloodshed and horror can be enacted any moment by sheer religious fanaticism and hate are blatantly before us in many parts of the world. The media loudly point them out almost every day. This is a dangerous situation in the atomic age.

If religion cannot bring harmony and, by its very nature, tends to form a ground for discord among human beings, as has been the case so far, then it cannot be a natural impulse healthy for survival. In this case, it can only be treated as a man-created way of life and thought. But the phenomenon has been wrongly interpreted and this wrong interpretation has been at the bottom of religious wars, crusades, forced conversions, persecutions, witch-hunts, oppressions, massacres, suffering and torture that fill the pages of history for the past thousands of years. What has happened before is happening even now before our eyes and can happen again. But what did not exist before is the possibility of total destruction of the race with the sophisticated weapons of our day. If mankind has to survive, not only political dissension but also religious discord must cease.

But how can this concord be brought about? The only way, in my opinion, is for science to locate the factors responsible for enlightenment. The illuminated founders of all faiths were human beings. They were born and had bodies like others. What mystery lay behind their extraordinary visions, the power of their words and the tremendous influence they exerted on countless human beings constitutes a riddle that has not been rationally answered so far.

The learned have no solution to this problem. From my point of view, there cannot be a more rational, more healthy and more efficacious method for achieving harmony among different faiths than the discovery of the natural law behind illumination and mystical ecstasy or the Revelations that came through them.

Mystical vision, enlightenment and prophethood are the natural endowments of a more evolved human brain brought in tune with the spiritual realities of the universe. I believe dogmatic barriers to the acceptance of this position will gradually cease, when the organic factors responsible for this transformation are clearly demonstrated by the objective methods of science. Sundry irrational beliefs and dogmas of faith continue to exist, on the one side, and skeptics continue to harangue against religion, on the other, because the Law is still unknown.

The extremists on both sides are sure to be silenced when it is objectively proved that religious feeling is a natural state in human beings, a born companion of the intellect to moderate its egoistic ardor and to help in the evolution of the brain till a personality proportionately balanced, both on the spiritual and intellectual sides, is formed.

This mystical feeling is almost always present in the intelligent human mind. Most of the outstanding geniuses in science, including Newton and Einstein, as also great poets and philosophers possessed this feeling to a pronounced degree. Illumination is the final product of this religious impulse and depends on a hitherto unlocated activity of the brain.

CHAPTER 2

The Mystical State—A More Evolved Form of Consciousness

I n the highest states of mystical ecstasy every object springs to life and the whole of Nature becomes alive. One incredible living, feeling Ocean of Being connects the mystic with every object in the universe. Mystical ecstasy is not an altered state of consciousness. It is not normal human consciousness in a state of rapture, or intense absorption in the contemplation of one object, or of quietude in which the mind reflects only a serene and silent state of awareness. It is in no way akin to the mental conditions produced by LSD, nitrous oxide, hypnosis or biofeedback or any other artificial method or chemical reagent.

There is no class of books that has been preserved with such love and care and regarded with such veneration as the gospels of every faith. They are considered sacred because what they deal with has been extremely rare and the subject they discuss is unfamiliar to the discursive intellect.

The teachings contained in the various scriptures took time to spread, for the seeds had to take root in the soil of the human mind. This is the reason why scriptural teaching has persisted and will continue to persist as long as the need exists in the subconscious depths of the human psyche. It is only in the genuine mystical experience that Revelation can occur. The ideas expressed and the language used in Revelation are inspired. They emanate from a higher dimension of consciousness, manifested only in an extremely limited number of cases through the course of history. This fact has been known for the past thousands of years. That is the reason why the gospels of a faith are held to be sacrosanct.

The present-day documents on the, so-called, altered states of consciousness only confuse the issue. What state of mind do they actually try to represent? If it is mystical experience, most of them deplorably fall short of the actual position. Mystical vision has nothing to do with sorcery, magic, miraculous happenings, weird adventures in the realm of the paranormal, bizarre visionary experiences or fantasies of any kind. In the genuine illuminative state there is no clouding of the intellect, no riot of colors, no encounters with strange creatures, no weird or bizarre scenes but only an indescribable state of glory, happiness and love, coupled with the direct experience of an All-Pervading Extended Consciousness or an Almighty, Omnipresent Cosmic Being.

The only sources available to gain correct and precise information about this state are the religious scriptures and the writings of the great mystics of the world. Since illuminated consciousness, and not altered consciousness, is the goal of human evolution, it is of utmost importance to make a distinction between the works of mystics and the fanciful, highly colored or sensational narratives of those who wish to create an applauding gallery for themselves or who mistakenly believe that they have the experience without making any attempt to confirm their belief. The distinction is necessary to protect the readers from mistaking one for the other. It is also very necessary to protect the image of the true mystical vision from distortion by the ambitious or the dabbler or the uninformed. It does not matter if the wrong portrayal is from a capable writer or the book has sold in millions of copies, it will die its own death if not based on the genuine experience. Nature has her own methods for sifting the true from the false. In course of time the human mind itself rejects what is not true or of lasting worth to it.

It is a unique experience of which the overwhelming impact has been described by most mystics in diverse ways. *The Cloud of Unknowing*, a well-known classic of spiritual life, compares it to a beam of ghostly light, piercing the cloud of unknowing that interposes between man and God. Augustine, quoted by Eckhart, likens it to being struck by lightning, when one hears inwardly the affirmation "Truth" to put a seal of authenticity on the experience.

St. Paul fell in a swoon on the road to Damascus and Moses experienced it as a fire in the bush. Mohammed saw himself carried on a winged horse, called Buraq, to the near Presence of God, and the experience had an overwhelming effect on his whole life. In one instant of Grace, Buddha realized that he was enlightened. A long period of life spent before that in austerity and religious practices brought forth no result comparable to this flash.

According to the papyri found in Egypt, Jesus is reported to have said: "Let him not who seeks cease until he finds, and when he finds he shall be astonished. Astonished he shall reach the Kingdom, and having reached the Kingdom he shall rest."

One of the Upanishads compares Brahman to a thunderbolt upraised ruling all the elements of creation. The Sufi

Bullah Shah, sings, "To ascend the gallows is the Pathway that leads to the love of the Lord. If you desire to have His vision, be ever prepared to wager your life for His sight."

The *Bhagavad Gita* graphically describes the impact of the vision in these lines:

> If the splendor of a thousand suns were to blaze out together, in the sky, that might resemble the glory of the Mahatman. There Pandava (Arjuna) beheld the whole universe, divided into manifold parts, standing in one in the body of the Deity of Deities. Then he, Arjuna, overwhelmed with astonishment, his hair standing on end, bowed down his head to the Shining One, and with joined palms spoke.

In every case of illumination, mere visionary experience is not sufficient. It must be attended by certain objective signs to confirm it.

Why has mystical vision such a powerful impact on the mind of the beholder that he often becomes intoxicated with the love of God, prefers solitude to even the most joyous company, renounces the ordinary pleasures of life to revel in a delight before which all the pleasures of the earth seem stale to him? What is there in this experience that it often over-comes earthly desires and ambitions and transmutes an in-dividual into a passionate lover, prepared to face severest trials and tribulations, agonizing torture and even death cheerfully for the sake of the beloved?

How can we explain the amazing psychological transfor-mation that brings unity in the multiplicity of the universe, shows One in All and All in One, or, in other words, the whole universe contained in the One Almighty Source of all? So far as I know, no rational explanation has been provided for this vision covering all the facets of the experience. It has to be remembered that in the mystical ecstasy the intellect remains active. There is no blunting of the rational faculty. This is repeatedly mentioned in the Upanishads. Reason has to be satisfied that the experience is not a delusion. This means that the vision is real. But, then, how can we account for it?

CHAPTER 3

Mystical Experience
And Psychic Energy

Our difficulty in explaining the nature of mystical experience stems mainly from the fact that we are not able to visualize a state of consciousness superior to our own. We cannot even imagine the state of mind of a musical or mathematical genius. A child cannot imagine the mind of an adult. We can understand the position better if we suppose that consciousness has an infinite series of gradations from the most strong to the most dilute. This we can illustrate by treating our own consciousness as the faint glimmer shed by a spark of fire and comparing it with the blinding glare of the gigantic surface of the sun. The human eye cannot even bear the sight of this splendor. It would be struck blind even when millions of miles away. Our consciousness is an extremely dilute form of this splendor.

Another analogy would be to liken our mind to a droplet of water and to compare it to an Ocean of Life. If this one small droplet of Divine Intelligence in man has been able to create the present amazing world of art, philosophy, science and the wonders of technology, what is impossible for the Almighty Ocean itself? What is there to prevent us from conceptualizing the truth that the whole universe, with its millions of galaxies and billions of suns and planets, is the creation of an Infinite Intelligence so concentrated that but one highly diluted atom suffices for all the mental activity of man?

We are not able to perceive this Almighty Intelligence or its Splendor because our sensory equipment is designed the other way. In fact, we are held prisoners by our brain. We are not able by any means to look into the mind of another person, as we look into a material object. Any mind other than our own is a completely unknown territory to us. Each one of the seven billion human minds, dwelling now on the earth, is an enchanted island invisible to the rest. There is no instrument that can see, measure, touch, smell or taste consciousness. Then how can we be conscious of Universal Consciousness, even if all our life we live, sleep, think and act in it?

This explains why mystical ecstasy has such an over-whelming impact on the mind. The visionary, for the first time, perceives the all-surpassing Splendor of Cosmic Intelligence. This is also the reason why intellect and science are both lost in the labyrinth of matter, for they look at the universe, as it were, through a filtering glass. The veil before our eyes is the creation of our senses. They act only within a particular range. Areas beyond that range are completely shut out from us. For instance, we cannot perceive the electromagnetic waves with any of our senses, but only through instruments and devices designed for the purpose.

Even our instruments, at this stage, cannot predict an earthquake, though some forms of life can sense in advance the coming shocks. A moth can smell its mate from even as far off as seven miles and a shark can scent blood two miles away. A bloodhound can detect the scent of an absconding criminal for scores of miles among thousands of other scents left by animals and human beings that walk over the same path. Bees find their way by polarized light imperceptible to human beings, and whales locate their prey with sonar-echo thousands of feet below the surface of the ocean. What worlds are hidden from us we cannot even imagine. For all we know, our sensory equipment might be but one set peculiar to the earth out of millions operative on other planets and other planes of creation in the universe.

We are mystified by U.F.O.'s and the psychic phenomena, because we are not prepared to concede that there are other planes of creation and other beings whose bodies are formed of other materials invisible to us. Mystical experience, in an instant, shatters the illusion that our subjective and objective worlds are the only actual realities.

In the mystical state a new element dominates the whole scene. The world of awareness and the world of matter fuse into one, a stupendous Consciousness now penetrates and encompasses all in a blaze of glory impossible to describe. As the Vision unfolds itself, the whole universe seems to melt in the splendor of the One present everywhere.

In order to understand mystical ecstasy in its true proportion, it is necessary to mark the difference between the animal and the human mind. The animal mind is extremely restricted and has absolutely no awareness of the world of knowledge, thought, imagination and feeling existing in man. It has absolutely no idea of science, mathematics, philosophy, poetry, literature, medicine, music, painting and sculpture which, all together, comprise a whole world entirely out of the reach of any other form of life on the earth.

The Real Nature of Mystical Experience

How has man taken this prodigious leap over the brute? How has the new world opened in him? Obviously, by the addition of more brain matter and a difference in the quality and configuration of the brain. We are told that the reptilian and animal brains still survive in man. Be that as it may, it is clear that the undoubted superiority of the mind of man over that of the animal is primarily due to the superiority of the human brain. Dolphins, too, have large brains and, as is well known, they are among the most intelligent creatures, below man, on earth.

Here we come to a crucial point in our discussion. So far as science is concerned, the human brain is a sealed compartment and has no other potentiality present in it over and above those manifested so far. This is an error and, as long as we continue to hold this view, the phenomena of mystical consciousness and extrasensory perception will continue to be unsolvable riddles for mankind.

We have seen what a tremendous change the addition of some ounces of brain matter has made in the life of man as compared to that of animals. But the mere quantitative or qualitative change in the brain does not explain the whole story. Dolphins, with an almost parallel brain weight, bear little comparison to man. Some small species of monkeys have proportionately larger brains than human beings. The ant with its tiny brain has an organizing capacity and a social order which is amazing. Science is still at sea so far as the phenomenon of life is concerned.

A Max Planck or an Einstein in the science of mind is needed to correct the error of the mechanistic interpreters of life. It is not elements of matter, like carbon, oxygen, calcium, hydrogen and others or the DNA and RNA molecules

15

alone of which life forms are compounded, but there is another element in nature, imperceptible to our senses, which is at the bottom of all phenomena of life. We can call it by the name of life-energy. It is this force which is credited with magical or miraculous powers in all the occult systems of the past and is known by various names, such as astral light, odic force, psychic energy, orgone, super-solar force, chi, etc. In India, it is known as *prana*, and has been universally held to be the lever behind mystical vision and paranormal gifts for the last more than three thousand years.

Prana can well be the matrix from which even physical energy is born. It might be present in the atom and sub-nuclear particles without ever being detected by any means known to science. It is, no doubt, a galling position, but it is true. The *pranic* force, in combination with atoms and molecules, fashions the bricks as also the complex structure of life. For this reason, it has been held to be the architect of the organic kingdom and the driving force behind evolution.

The Power of the Creator that brings the universe into existence is known as *Shakti* in India. *Shakti* is mind and matter both. Gnosis or Knowledge comes from the Creator. This is the Divine Spark or Soul in us—the Inner Light that illumines the mind and the intellect both.

We sometimes become aware of this real "Knower" in states of deep contemplation or in the impartial Self which tells us that we are wrong, when, in the heat of anger or passion or in any other turbulent mental state or disturbed reason, we wrongly act or think. It is this Self or *atman*, as it is named in the *Upanishads*, which becomes more clear and perceptible in the mystical state.

Shakti, as the Power of the Creator, is incomprehensible

16

to the intellect. We are already at the frontier, in the investigation of matter and mind both, where the unfathomable nature of the deeper layers of creation, with the tools available to us in the form of our senses and the mind, is becoming increasingly apparent to the leading scientists and thinkers of our day. *Shakti* is unconditioned and limitless, capable of creating any kind of world or substance one can conceive of or that is inconceivable. *Prana*, too, is a form of *Shakti*. It is the Energy behind the phenomena of life. It is the Power behind faith-healing and miracles, as also behind time, space or causality, also emptiness, timelessness and chaos.

What amazing worlds, what incredible forms of life and what unimaginable planes of existence it has created or will create, we can never know. The dream state is a distant sample to show its bewildering play. It is *maya*, the incomprehensible and unexplainable illusory power of the Creator, which our intellect can never entirely understand. The theory of relativity, the progressive discovery of sub-nuclear particles, with amazing properties, and the new finds of black holes, pulsars, quasars, the expanding universe and anti-matter all point to the conclusion that, with every advance in knowledge gained so far, the universe has not become simpler and easier to understand, but more complex and more difficult to grasp by the intellect.

To what undreamed of conclusions the investigation done by science will lead, in the course of even one century, no one can predict. Indian metaphysics is based on the experience of *samadhi* or mystical vision. In this state, the subtle worlds of mind and *prana* become perceptible to the Yogi. In the time to come, science will have to adopt the same methods to reach these transcendent planes. There is no other way for man to find other areas of creation not perceptible to our senses. It is only then that the true proportion of creation can be understood by the human mind.

At present, we deal only with the fraction perceptible to us. The longing for spiritual experience exists even in the most intelligent minds, because there is always a subconscious sense of insufficiency in the physical knowledge gained and of emptiness in one's knowledge of the self.

Prana is the bewildering source behind the amazing organizations and instincts of living creatures. With the first breakthrough in the discovery of *prana*—which is imminent now—the incredible behavior of the intellect that has persisted in ascribing the phenomenon of life and evolution to pure unpremeditated chance will at once become apparent.

There is a different spectrum of *prana* for each form of life, with modifications for each individual of that form. We know very well that the organic structures and their chemical compositions in every species of life vary from each other, and there are slight differences in the individuals of each species. This is true of *prana* also. Each distinct human personality reflects a distinct type of *pranic* spectrum. No two spectrums are alike in every respect, as there are no two personalities similar in every way.

The differences in our mental constitutions and character are all due to variations in the spectrum of *prana* of each individual. In the *pranic* plane, human personalities exist as clear and distinct as their mortal frames in the physical world. During the course of mystical ecstasy, a new, more potent stream of *prana* enters the brain, creating a revolution in consciousness. The flow of this new *pranic* current is caused by a slight but clearly marked activity in the brain. It looks as if a hitherto silent area has leapt to a sudden activity, demanding a more potent psychic fuel to sustain it.

When the available store of this new *pranic* fuel is spent, the mystic again reverts to his normal consciousness, returning, as it were, from a smiling, brightly lit Garden of Paradise to the humdrum existence of a prosaic world. No words can express the grandeur and sublimity of the experience nor the happiness and serenity felt during the interval. In rare cases, the experience can become a perennial feature of human life. In India, it has been called the *sahaja* or *jivan-mukta* state.

The whole ocean of *prana*, sustaining the human race, is in a state of flux. It is this motion of the fundamental element of life which is behind the evolution of the brain and transformation of consciousness. The human world is advancing in knowledge because *prana* is moving in that direction. This movement, in turn, causes subtle evolutionary changes in the brain which we are not able to measure yet but will do so when the mystery shrouding *prana* is solved. This will also solve the riddle of talent, genius and extrasensory perception for a well-marked change in *prana* is responsible for these conditions, too.

The evolutionary change occurring in the race now is irresistible. Mankind is being carried to an, at present, unknown destination by the very ocean of life which feeds every individual mind night and day. This destination is a new dimension of consciousness which has not been previously defined so far. We call it by the name of mystical experience, illumination or enlightenment without knowing precisely what that means. All of us are sailing in the same mysterious ship without knowing for which port it is bound.

Chapter 4

My Own Experience
Of the Mystical State

I do not claim to be illuminated in the sense we ascribe illumination to Buddha, as I still find myself at the human level. I do not claim to be a prophet in the sense of the Founders of various faiths, as I do not find myself equal to the task they set out to accomplish. I do not claim to be a mystic or a saint, as I am still very much entrenched in the world and have not completely risen above it.

I feel more at home in calling myself a normal human being, like millions of others who inhabit the earth. It gives me even greater happiness, when I measure the difference between my frail human self and the surpassing glory of the Vision granted to me.

All that I claim is that, for the last more than forty years, I have been undergoing a most extraordinary experience which is now a constant source of wonder and joy to me. The experience is not at all like anything I tasted of life from the day I began to remember, as a child, to my thirty-fourth year. It is not like anything of science or art or philosophy of which I have read to this day. The only class of human beings in whom I find a parallel of this experience are the mystics of the East and the West, but here, too, are differences which I am trying my best to resolve.

In describing this experience, I always thoroughly weigh every word that I use, as somehow I feel myself under a solemn obligation to give expression to what is the strictest truth. But, even so, my whole story is so incredible that doubt is natural unless direct proof is provided to substantiate it. I and my friends are seriously occupied, at this moment, in finding methods for an objective verification of this almost unbelievable mental state.

But, as long as that does not become possible, the only evidence I can provide is the voluminous store of all the mystical literature of the world, covering the last more than 3,500 years. To a modern psychologist, from the point of view of normalcy, I am a freak or a victim to a permanently fixed delusory state. He is not to blame. There are no documentaries of cases of this kind. I myself disbelieved the evidence of my own senses and mind for as long as twelve years, when, suddenly, an objective fact brought it home to me that the transformation I was undergoing was not a delusion but a concrete reality to which I had to reconcile myself.

The incredible nature of my transformation lies in this, that every moment of my life I live in two worlds. One is the sensory world which we all share together—the world of sight, touch, smell, taste and sound. My reactions to this world are the same as of other human beings. The other is an amazing super-sensory world to which I first found entrance in 1937, and which, to the best of my knowledge, I share alone, or, perhaps, with extremely few others unknown to me. I do not say this to claim singularity, but only as a statement of fact, because to this day I have not come across

21

any individual claiming the same peculiarity. I have critically observed myself, my thoughts, my actions, my feelings and my dreams, to make sure that the transformation experienced is not an abnormality or an aberration but the normal outcome of a peculiar activity of my cerebrospinal system, unknown to modern science. I have talked about my condition with many scores of eminent scientists and scholars in different parts of the world. But the mystery and wonder still remain.

There is no explanation for my extraordinary mental condition. I am always conscious of a luminous glow not only in my interior, but pervading the whole field of my vision during the hours of my wakefulness. I literally live in a world of light. It is as if a light were burning in my interior, filling me with a luster so beautiful and so ravishing that my attention is again and again drawn towards it. In fact, it is the normal state of my perception now. Light, both within and without, and a distinct music in my ears, are the two prominent features of my transformed being.

It is as if, in my interior, I live in a charming, radiant and melodious world. A sense of its fascination is always present in me. The harmony is disturbed, more or less, in unhealthy states of the body in the same way as sickness disturbs the poise of the normal mind. The luster and the sounds continue but are no longer as fascinating as in the healthy state. This disturbance is only occasional. Normally an indwelling joy and harmony make my life much more happy and serene than it was before the transformation.

Experience of light is a prominent feature of mystical vision. This is sometimes described as a supernatural glow, ghostly light, celestial radiance, golden luster, living splendor, and the like. There is hardly any narrative of a mystical experience in which the glory, the brightness or the splendor of the vision is not mentioned at one place or the other. On the basis of my own experience, I can safely assert that the mystical vision, whether of a short or long duration, invariably denotes the operation of an altered form of psychic energy which is luminous, lending a brightness to every object perceived outside and to every image evoked within.

To sum up briefly, mystical experience represents, in my view, the activity of a luminous form of thought-energy which bathes everything in its luster. I believe that by a slow process of evolution this illuminated state of the mind, in course of time, will become the natural state of every man and woman on the earth.

The reason why the sun and the moon are used as symbols of illumination or of the attainment of miraculous powers in almost all the spiritual, esoteric, occult or hermetic traditions, is because of the resemblance of this inner radiance with the sources of light which illumine the earth. The current confusion about the real nature of mystical experience rests on the fact that there is no awareness about the biological factors responsible for this extraordinary state of cognition.

As soon as it is confirmed by experiment that a transformation does occur in the brain as also in the bioenergy which fuels the activity of thought, the speculations and controversies, circling round the subject at present, will cease, giving a new direction to the investigation of the phenomenon.

Mystical experience is the perception of this celestial luster as a crown of glory round the soul. This is what the *Hymn of the Robe of Glory* aims to convey in the song beginning with the words:

23

When a quiet little child, I was dwelling
In the House of my Father's Kingdom,
And in the wealth and the glories
Of my Upbringers I was delighting . . . .

The soul is deprived of this Robe of Glory on its embodiment as a human being. But it recovers this Mantle of Light with noble striving, when it attains the Illuminated State. This is also what William Blake aims to convey in the first stanza of his poem, "Song," which he wrote at an early age:

How sweet I roamed from field to field,
And tasted all the Summer's pride,
Till I the Prince of Love beheld
Who in the sunny beam did glide.

The Chinese sage, Wei-Lang, in his sutra about the indwelling Buddha, expresses the same idea in these lines:-

Within the domain of our mind there is a Tathagata
of Enlightenment who sends forth a powerful light
which illumines externally the six gates (of sensation) and purifies them. This light is strong enough
to pierce through the six heavens of desire, and
when it is turned inwardly to the Essence of Mind
it eliminates at once the three poisonous elements,
purges away our sins which lead us to the hells, and
enlightens us thoroughly within and without.

I do not claim that I see God, but I am conscious of a Living Radiance both within and outside of myself. In other words, I have gained a new power of perception, not present before. The luminosity does not end with my waking time. It persists even in my dreams. In every state of being—eating, drinking, talking, working, laughing, grieving, walking or sleeping—I always dwell in a rapturous world of light. It is obvious that the self or observer in me has experienced a change and a new being has been born who is always enwrapped in a sheath of alluring light.

If my experience were confined to the state of luminosity alone, I would, in all probability, have kept the secret to myself and not divulged it far and wide as something exceptional that deserved attention. But this inner radiance is attended by another even more incredible feature which, from my point of view, is of utmost importance and provides a possible solution to, at least, four still unsolved riddles of the human mind, namely: 1. mystical experience or illumination, 2. inspiration and genius, 3. psychic faculties, such as clairvoyance, telepathy, prophecy, etc., and 4. a whole gamut of mental and nervous disorders which can be defined and classified through a scientific study of the phenomenon.

The link between genius and insanity is well known. We have also a class of psychics, known as *mastanas* in Persian and *avadhoots* in Sanskrit, who are highly clairvoyant with abnormal behavior patterns. They can be found in mental clinics, if carefully looked for. This shows that the transformation that occurred in me could also go awry, as it did for some time. This has an awesome significance.

It means that human evolution, if not supported by a harmonious inner and outer environment, can result in malformations of the mind and intellect. This is the tragedy of our day. The more amazing feature of my experience consists in this: The enchanting light I perceive, both internally and outside, is alive. It pulsates with life and intelligence. It is like an infinite Ocean of Awareness pervading my own small pool of consciousness within and the whole universe I perceive with my senses, outside. It is as if a radiant living Presence encompasses everything that exists both within and outside of me. Much as I wish to do so, it is extremely difficult for me to draw a clear picture of this aspect of my experience. For me the universe is alive. A stupendous Intelligence, which I can sense but never fathom, looms behind every object and every event in the universe, silent, still, serene and, in the words of Bullah Shah, the Sufi of Punjab, immovable like a mountain.

It is a staggering spectacle. I can describe it only by a distant analogy. Imagine the universe as a gigantic movie, unfolding scene after scene, in time and space, on an infinitely vast, intensely alive ethereal screen, which remains entirely unaffected by the action of the drama, and you will have a dim picture of what I mean.

The mystics have likened this visionary experience of the behind-the-scenes Cosmic Intelligence to the motionless bed of an ocean supporting all the movement, fury and flurry of its agitated surface layer, which is the phenomenal world.

It would be a serious error to suppose that this all-pervading, behind-the-scenes Cosmic Intelligence is of the nature of human consciousness and human reason. It is not. It is something so remote from our conception and so extraordinary that nothing of this earth can provide an analogy to explain it.

It is for this reason that the phrase "Neti, Neti:" not this, not this, has been repeatedly used by the seers of the Upanishads to emphasize the utterly incommunicable nature of this experience.

The Sufis, too, have a graphic story to illustrate this point. The story runs that in a certain village there was a walled enclosure hiding a mystery. Whoever climbed the wall and looked on the other side jumped into the enclosure and never returned.

This made the villagers curious and they decided to try an experiment to prevent the climber from jumping over without revealing to them what he had seen. When the next candidate volunteered to climb, they firmly held him by the legs and pulled him back the moment he attempted to jump and disappear forever. But he had lost the power of speech and stared from one to the other without being able to utter a word. The moral is that mystical vision dumbfounds the keenest intellect.

Chapter 5

Mystical Vision the Basis of Religion

The attributes of "Omniscience," "Omnipotence" and "Omnipresence" ascribed to the Creator or God or Allah or Ishvara in the theistic religions of mankind, are all based on the impressions gathered during mystical ecstasy. The living Presence or Over-All Intelligence, now occupying the whole area of perception of the seer—the sky, the earth and the whole multitude of objects contained in them, the largest and the smallest—is so unimaginably all-pervasive that it seems to be doing everything at every place in every moment of time.

One Almighty Actor, One unbounded Ocean of Intelligence, One Infinite living Sun plays the whole Drama of Creation, singlehanded, manifest in every grain and particle in the microcosmic and every sun and planet in the macrocosmic plane of the universe. There is nothing startling or singular in what I am stating. This Unity of the Universe, this Oneness of the Cosmos is a most prominent feature of mystical experience.

Almost every great mystic has voiced it. The *Aitareya Upanishad* describes the experience in these words:

> He is Brahma, He is Indra, He is Praja-
> pati (Lord of the Universe). He is all these

> gods, and these five great elements, namely earth, air, ether, water, light, these things and those which are mingled of the fire, as it were, the seeds of one sort and another, those born from an egg, or those born from a womb, and those born from sweat, and born from a sprout, horses, cows, persons and elephants, whatever breathing thing that is here, whether moving or flying, or what is stationary, all this is guided by Intelligence, is established in Intelligence. The world is guided by Intelligence. The support is Intelligence. Brahma is Intelligence."

This passage is of tremendous importance. It is the outcome of true mystical experience which shows Consciousness as the bedrock of all creation, both animals and inanimate.

I have read through several accounts of mystical vision recorded by contemporary writers or intellectuals of our own day. A good many of them lack conviction and are but the products of the intellect. It is not merely a feeling of unity or oneness with creation or sense of euphoria that determines the mystical ecstasy. It is the overwhelming nature of the spectacle that shows consciousness and not the material universe as the dominating Reality.

The experience reverses one's whole concept of creation. The sun, the stars, the earth and its oceans are not now perceived as material realities but as images projected by an all-embracing Consciousness. In other words, the cognitive power of the brain is dramatically changed for the duration of the vision. A new channel of perception comes into operation. What was but a point of awareness before, inextricably linked to a body of flesh and bone, becomes the Ocean, enfolding the whole of the universe, while the body and the "ego" that made up the personality of the observer recede further and further away, leaving the way open for a Cosmic Intelligence to manifest itself.

It is important to remember that the experience is not of an impersonal kind. It is not as if we are witnessing an earthly scene. In the normal experience there always exist the duality of the "Knower" and the "Known," of the subjective mind and the objective world. This distinction persists even in dreams. Except in deep states of absorption or intense embrace of love, this sense of duality is an inalienable part of human awareness.

In the mystical ecstasy the very self is transfigured. It becomes the subject and the object both. The Titanic Presence that now dominates the scene is the whole universe and the soul of the individual at the same time. It is the sun and the atom both. This infinite Source of All dwells here in my heart with all the frailties or virtues I possess. This Cosmic Intelligence, this almighty Sovereign of all creation is, at the same time, the individual self of all the six billion earthly human beings, the actor in all the six billion dramas of life and billions upon billions of infinitely varied dramas on other planets in the universe, yet away and aloof from them all. It is a breathtaking experience.

The narrow individual self is swept off from its anchor in the body and the world, like a straw carried away by a tidal wave of the ocean, to be confronted by Infinity on every side.

This is what Rumi tries to convey in the *Dewan-I-Shamsi Tabrez* in these lines: "Having put Duality aside, the two worlds (this world and the other) are now one to me.

It is One I seek, One I know, One I see and One I call." The well-known mystic William Law describes this experience of Oneness of Soul with the Infinite in these words:

> Though God is everywhere present, yet He is only present to thee in the deepest and most central part of the soul. The natural senses cannot possess God or unite thee to Him, nay, the inward faculties of understanding, will and memory can only reach after God, but cannot be the place of His habitation in thee. But there is root or depth in thee from whence all these faculties come forth, as lines from a center, or as branches from the body of the tree. This depth is called the center, the fund or bottom of the soul. This depth is the unity, the eternity— I had almost said the infinity of thy soul—for it is so infinite that nothing can satisfy it or give it rest but the infinity of God.

Shankaracharya sums up the position in this way:

> The verdict of all discussions on the Vedanta is that the *jiva* (soul) and the whole of the universe are nothing but Brahman, and that liberation means abiding in Brahman, the indivisible entity. The *Shrutis* themselves are authority (for the statement) that Brahman is One without a Second.

In recent times, Dr. Bucke's experience, described in his book, *Cosmic Consciousness*, is clearly illustrative of the cognitive state in mystical ecstasy:

31

Directly afterwards, there came upon me a sense of exaltation, of immense joyousness, accompanied or immediately followed by an intellectual illumination quite impossible to describe ... Among other things I did not come to believe, I saw and knew that the Cosmos is not dead matter, but a living Presence, that the soul of man is immortal, that the universe is so built and ordered that without any peradventure all things work together for the good of each and all.

Woodsworth hints at in this well-known passage:

... something far more deeply interfused
Whose dwelling is the light of the setting suns,
And the round ocean, and the living air,
And the blue sky, and in the mind of man,
A motion and a spirit, that impels
All thinking things, all objects of all thought,
And rolls through all things.

An important saying of Christ, according to the Egyptian papyri is as follows:

...And the Kingdom of Heaven is within you and whosoever knoweth himself shall find it and, having found it, ye shall know yourselves that ye are sons and heirs of the Father, the Almighty, and shall know yourselves that ye are in God and God in you. And ye are the city of God.

This is one of the clearest statements to show that the human body is a Temple of the Divine and that the aim of human life is to experience this Divinity. But how can it be possible to achieve the Glorious Vision without transformation of the Self? Evolution is the only rational explanation for this ascent from the normal human perception to the paranormal state where the Kingdom of Heaven becomes a reality through the enhanced powers of our organic frame.

Chapter 6

Science and Mystical Experience

There is a great deal of variation in the accounts of mystical vision available to us for study. Apart from the traditional mystics, whose frame of mind was essentially religious and who underwent various spiritual disciplines to attain the mystical state, there have been poets, philosophers, scientists and scholars who had a sudden visionary experience, once or several times in their life, without the practice of any orthodox religious or esoteric discipline. Pascal, Bucke, Tennyson, Wordsworth and Tagore are a few examples of this type of mystical vision. According to his own statement, a few moments before his epileptic seizures, Dostoevsky experienced a state of lucidity and bliss which, he says, counted more than a lifetime of ordinary experience.

How are we to account for this phenomenon? From immemorial times the mystical state has been held to be a vision of Divinity, or God or Allah or Brahman or any celestial or supernatural Being. There are hundreds of books from the pens of mystics themselves or of theologians and other scholars supporting this view. For this reason a deeply religious life, involving seclusion from the world, renunciation, submission to Divine Will, contentment, austerity, even penance with extreme love of the Deity, and utter devotion, has been considered to be the essential prerequisite for success in this sublime quest. The Revealed scriptures of mankind are all explicit on this point. From this point of view, the anomaly created by the mystical ecstasy of those on whom the experience was, as it were, thrust in the course of normal life, devoted to worldly pursuits, without having made the surrenders and sacrifices to deserve the reward from Heaven, is hard to explain.

There have been well-known mystics in recent times in whom ecstasy started from boyhood, as in the case of Ramakrishna and Ramana Maharshi. In both of them the state of intense absorption was, as it were, a natural state of the mind. Guru Nanak and Jnaneshwar were mystics from birth. The former in his talk, behavior and poetic composition was a religious genius from the age of ten, while the latter wrote his famous commentary on the *Bhagavad Gita* known as Jnaneshwari, and considered to be a classic, at the age of sixteen. There is no rational explanation for these extraordinary cases of mystical consciousness.

There are still many scientists who, like Freud, treat the whole phenomenon of religion as an illusion, a pathological condition due to repressed sexuality—their one answer to many problems of the mind. According to this view, the whole irrational fabric of faith should have been exposed to its bottom by now. But, strange to say, the reverse has happened. Mystical vision and the miracles associated with it, now classified as psychic phenomena, have assumed an urgency and importance that they never possessed before during the last two centuries.

This shows how erroneous the intellect can be. The widespread thirst for self-awareness or the occult side of nature, which is a striking feature of our day, is utterly inexplicable in the light of modern psychology. It is incredible that the learned world should still be in the dark about a phenomenon that has been at the base of civilization and culture, also all the moral and intellectual progress made by mankind. The religious impulse and the lure of the supernatural, which we see always associated with the life of man from as far back as archeological record is available, provide irrefutable evidence to show that the human mind has been occupied with the occult and the divine almost from the beginning of reason.

The priest, the witch doctor, the medicine man and the shaman appear on the scene from the remotest periods. In the prehistorical world we see all the vanished civilizations of the past completely dominated by religion. In fact, in some of them the kings performed the offices of the ruler and the high priest both.

The current faiths that took form from about 2,000 years before the birth of Christ to medieval times kept as firm a hold on the imagination of man as those that preceded them by thousands of years. In this sphere of the human mind, science is but a helpless spectator of the scene.

The world is tense and the race lives under the overhanging threat of a holocaust because we are violating an Almighty Law of nature. We have not even the awareness of this Law. It is not mere chance or accident or hysteria or the machinations of charlatans and priests that brought the current major faiths of mankind into existence. In such an event, they could never hold the tremendous sway which they did over the minds of people in almost all parts of the world. It is not by chance or accident that the great spiritual luminaries were born to reveal the mode of life and the pattern of behavior to be followed by the multitude to live in concord with the evolutionary processes working in the race.

It is the impact of their teachings and the order they established which prepared the soil for the great achievements of modern science. The parents, grandparents and the great-grandparents of the pioneers of science were, in most cases, deeply religious men and women with faith in God and a righteous way of life. What will be the achievements of the progeny, born in all parts of the world, two or three generations from now, in the mental climate which undiluted rationality has created we have still to see.

The signs, however, are not auspicious. Pregnancy and birth in a tense, highly charged and threatened mental atmosphere can never be above fault. The tragedy has been that the custodians of faith attached more importance to formulism than to the basic teachings of the founders.

At the same time, many of the great thinkers and scientists, during recent times, failed to understand the importance of religion as the outward symbol of the deeply rooted evolutionary impulse in human beings. They failed to note that all the revealed scriptures of mankind had a common purpose which is to implant an ideal of a Heavenly Deity, called by the name of Brahman, God, Jehovah, Vishnu, Allah, Buddha or Ahura-Mazda, etc., and, to prescribe the way of life and the mode of behavior necessary to achieve union with or proximity to that Being. In other words, the aim was to present an evolutionary ideal and the methods to achieve it. Religion came, as I have said, to prepare the ground for science. The advent of science, too, did not come by chance or accident. It marks another stage in the evolution of the human mind. We do not see the connection because there persists an erroneous impression, even in the ranks of science, that the human brain is static and has been so for the last, at least, twenty thousand years, since the time of the Cro-Magnon type of man.

We are, however, prepared to concede that there must have been some kind of a qualitative difference between the brain of a genius, as for instance Einstein, and a man of average intelligence. In fact, it is to locate this difference that portions of Einstein's brain have been under observation for the last many years.

The wonder is that while we are ready to acknowledge that there must be a variation in the brain of a genius as compared to that of a common man, we still naively believe the myth that there has been no appreciable change in the human encephalon for the past thousands of years. Even a champion of evolution, like Teilhard-de-Chardin, subscribed to the same view, probably under the impression that what the biologists of his day propounded was the last word on the subject. The bloom of science and the bloom of intellect, we see today, compared to the dense, slow-moving mind of the Stone Age man, shows as great a gulf, if not greater, as exists between a highly talented individual and a blockhead in our time.

What physiological factors are responsible for this difference? No one is able to answer this riddle at present. The moment this difference is located, the enigma whether or not the human brain is still in a state of evolution will be solved.

The tragedy is that the human mind is never able to frame a correct picture of the state of its knowledge even a few decades ahead. The great intellects, alive in the late

1800's, could never imagine the state of knowledge of the intellects alive today. Similarly, the latter can never visualize correctly the mind of those living in the late 2000's. There are extremely few who can think ahead of their time. The science of life has reached a stage where a breakthrough in our knowledge about the brain is imminent. This would show that the religious impulse is genetically present in human beings. Where it does not exist, a departure from the normal is indicated.

The aim of the impulse is to effect coordination between the evolutionary modeling of the body and the surface consciousness of the individual. I say this because there is no other explanation for mystical experience. The fact that those who laid the foundation of all current faiths of mankind made a clear avowal of the position that what they were preaching was revealed to them by God, or an Angel, or a Divine Consciousness, or an Enlightened state of mind is a clear indication of this fact.

With the breakthrough in the knowledge about the brain, the stage will be set for rapprochement between religion and science. The real purpose for which science took birth is to bring about an acceleration in the evolution of mankind. From this point of view, science is not the end but the means to an end. This is the reason for the highly increased tempo of progress in our time.

We are all a witness to the fact that changes and innovations that, in medieval times, took centuries to occur are often accomplished in decades now. How has this come to pass? The answer that this is due to highly sophisticated technology is only partially correct. Technology itself is inextricably linked up with the capacity of the human mind.

It is the technological brain that has evolved to the pitch where the amazing achievements of our day have become possible. If the evolution of the brain does not keep pace with the speed of progress, a state of stagnation would ensue beyond which it would be impossible to proceed. The past history of mankind is standing witness to this ossification. What happened to the Egyptians, Mesopotamians, the people of the Indus Valley, the Indo-Aryans, Chinese, Persians, Greeks and Romans after their rise to lofty heights of culture and even technological achievements of which we see surprising relics even today? Stultification and decadence occurred as the brain ceased to keep pace with the demands of the progress achieved, and decay set in to level the once victorious and ascendant nations to dust.

As many as fourteen civilizations, whose achievements are scattered all over the earth, which, some believe, were harvests of their contact with extraterrestrial intelligence, have already paid the forfeit for their ignorance of this Almighty Law. Our civilization will follow the same course, if science continues to ignore the fact that spiritual evolution is the real goal of human life.

The time-defying pyramids and the wonder-exciting temples of Egypt could not save the populace from falling a helpless victim to decline, when the brain ceased to cooperate. Space rockets, skyscrapers and all the wonders of modern science, combined, will not be able to save the race, if the brain refuses to tolerate the pressure to which it is subjected now, because of ignorance of the Law. The result would be what we are already witnessing—a desire to drop out of the struggle, perverted thinking, drugs, promiscuity, escapism, discontent, violence, crime and wishful thinking of a holocaust. The top-heavy, ponderous structure of modern civilization, in every part of the world is actually rocking. Only we are not fully aware of it, as we are not conscious of the worldwide rebellious trend of the human brain.

Chapter 7

The Need for
A Serious Study of the Phenomenon

I n dealing with mystical ecstasy we deal with a fundamental impulse in the human mind. Modern science has absolutely no awareness of the fact that the average human brain, as the result of continued evolution, is now ripe for the manifestation of another mode of cognition superior to the intellect. It is only through this channel that Consciousness can be perceived as an independent Reality existing in a boundless universe of its own.

It is the emergence of this cognitive faculty which the ancient Indian adepts designated as the opening of the "Third Eye," or the "Tenth Door," and the Egyptians represented by the symbol of the Serpent on the headdress of Pharaohs, by the "Eye of Horus" and other emblems. The whole occult, esoteric, hermetic and alchemic literature of mankind evolves round this amazing possibility in the human brain.

The phenomenon of mystical ecstasy has not received the attention it deserves on the part of empiricists, because the possibility in the brain is not even suspected. There is no awareness about the forces behind psychokinetic phenomena or extrasensory perception, nor about what relation they bear to the brain of the psychic or medium who displays the gifts. The possibility in the involvement of the brain in the weird demonstrations is not even mentioned as a subject for discussion. But almost every saint or mystic has been credited with psychic gifts and some mystics are reported to have exhibited these gifts to a remarkable extent.

The life-stories of saints throughout the world often contain accounts of their miraculous performances. How are we able to account for them? Patanjali, the author of the first authoritative treatise on Yoga, who flourished centuries before the birth of Christ, treats psychic or miraculous gifts as an inevitable harvest of yogic discipline and divides them into eight categories.

There is close affinity between the practice of Yoga and the disciplines followed by Sufis, Christian mystics and the Taoists of China. The exercises are directed to train and discipline all the constituents of the human personality—imagination, will, thought, emotion, as also the physical body. Concentration and self-mastery constitute the pivotal exercises. Discipline and mental training have been considered necessary for illumination or the attainment of miraculous powers from immemorial times.

Why? Has any rational explanation been offered to show why mental and physical discipline is necessary for religious experience or psychic gifts? Are the mental exercises and the ennoblement of character undertaken to propitiate a Divine Power to win favor?

If the answer is in the affirmative, it means that divine intervention is needed as a necessary condition for enlightenment. In that case, the phenomenon of mystical ecstasy must always remain beyond the periphery of science. The same must then be the position of psychic powers also. How can then the research that is now being done on psychic phenomena lead to any tangible results, when the energies and forces involved are purely subjective, operating as it were, in a magical way, without any relationship to the human organism? If this position does not accord with the law-bound character of the universe, and there must be a rational explanation behind the repeatedly observed fact of spiritual illumination or the possession of psychic faculties, it is necessary then to look more closely into the personality of man to find an answer to this riddle.

Intellectual speculation or scientific study of the subject can never help one cross the barrier and understand the nature of mystical consciousness. The empiricist who would like to explore this territory must experiment in the laboratory of his own self. Nature has built an unscalable wall here to keep the intellect from intruding into a territory that belongs to a superior sense. If this wall did not exist, reason would continue to dominate the mind of man and the emergence of a higher faculty would never be possible. The natural function of intellect is to help this evolution.

Just as it is not humanly possible to arrest the normal growth of adulthood of a healthy child, except at the risk of malformation and distortion, in the same way, it is not possible to block the evolution of the human mind except by causing malformation and distortion of the whole personality. In the case of isolated savage populations in Africa, Australia and the new world, cannibalistic practices and human sacrifices and other perverse and inhuman customs were the result of obstructed evolution. Correction and reformation came when the obstructions were removed. At the present stage of human progress, any obstruction in the path of evolution can be disastrous. The slightest abnormality, twist or kink in even a few of the leading intellects of a nation, especially a powerful nation, can prove calamitous for the whole race. We have to bear in mind that the two bloodiest wars in all history have already been fought in this century.

Apart from them, a whole chain of appalling massacres in different countries spelled the death of scores of millions of innocent human beings, dwarfing all the bloody slaughters of the past. In the light of what has already happened, deluded, indeed, is the intellect which fails to draw a lesson from these happenings of the twentieth century and lives unconcerned about the future. It is good to be optimistic, but heedlessness is a sign of mental inertia highly inimical to survival.

Since it is hard to accept that an All-knowing Intelligence controls the destiny of mankind, we are prone to ascribe the present overhanging threat of a global war and the precarious condition of the world to a chance combination of certain factors or to a rapid advance in technology and entertain the hope that the crisis would pass off with a proper handling of the situation by the political leadership of mankind. But we never ascribe it to the imbalance created by disproportionate growth of the human personality—a giant intellect attended by a pigmy will and a dwarf moral conscience.

Survey all the departments of human activity and the truth of this statement will become obvious to you. The reason for the menacing condition of the present world lies in the imminent danger of disproportionate evolution which, if not corrected, would be fatal for the race.

It is the racial consciousness, prescient of the pernicious outcome of this disproportion in the nuclear age, sounding warning after warning at the heedless crowd. In the mystical

45

state, where there occurs a more direct contact with Cosmic Consciousness, the warning comes as a Message or an inspired composition to draw attention to the digression. This is the secret behind the prophetic utterances and the predictions of upcoming disasters, made by prophets, oracles and seers, throughout the past and, in our time, by clairvoyants like Edgar Cayce and a few others.

Chapter 8

The Divine in Man
And How to Achieve It

E very human being is a ray of the Light Divine. This is what every man and woman needs to know and experience in themselves. This is the glorious Prize which every one of us has come to win. This is the Message which, in my own humble way, I have come to deliver. There is nothing new in this Message. It is written in bold letters and couched in forceful language in all the religious scriptures of mankind. I stand before you as a living testimony to the truth of religion and an eyewitness to the experiences undergone by all the great visionaries, illuminated sages and mystics of the past.

I became a recipient of this Grace by a series of transformations which occurred with great pain and suffering for years. This gave me a clue to the biological factors responsible for the change. Why I was chosen for the experiment I do not know. This is a wonder and a mystery to me. I had no special merit to deserve the favor.

Perhaps, heredity played a more decisive role in this transformation than my own efforts. The laws of Spirit have to be followed by the parent and the offspring both. It is only then that the Path of Evolution can become easy and smooth to travel for the human race. Earth-wide dissemination of knowledge of the Glory dwelling in every human being is the only way to bring about the unification of all mankind. It will make known the common Goal prescribed by nature for the life of man. The solemn task in front of us is to provide empirical evidence for the basic reality of Illumination.

This is absolutely necessary to bridge the existing gulf between religion and science, and to bring concord between the intellect and heart of man. This is also needed to convince the skeptic and to clear the doubts of the vacillating. Also to confirm the belief of the believer and to show the true Path to the seeker, thus correcting the error of the superstitious and the credulous dupe.

I firmly believe the time has come for this great reconciliation, and that nature has already set the stage for it. Those who have doubts should look towards the miracles of science, wrought by the intellect, and ask themselves whether there cannot be miracles of spirit also.

The knowledge of this priceless Treasure of the Spirit, far more precious than all the wealth and seats of power on the earth, can provide the most powerful incentive to all noble souls to search for it in themselves and to persuade others to make the rewarding search.

When empirically proved, it is sure to galvanize the whole race into activity to find the methods and to create the environment by which the effort made to win the Glorious Prize can be greatly facilitated. This is the only knowledge that can humble the powerful and the proud, enrich and embolden the poor and the weak; the only knowledge that can provide a most powerful incentive to parents to ennoble their lives and strengthen the bonds of their love to procreate an illuminated progeny. It can vindicate the stand of those who are already on the spiritual Path, and inspire those who are not. It can highly promote the benevolent efforts of those who, susceptible to the influence of the Spirit, are already engaged in activities aimed to bring peace, harmony and self-knowledge to the world, as also relief from sickness, suffering, pain and want to the needy crowds.

With the first objective confirmation of this divine potential in human beings, the wider areas of discord between contending political ideologies and the conflicting doctrines of faith will slowly begin to narrow down till complete accord is achieved. The convinced scientists and the scholars will be the first to take up the cry. Those who think that the dream is too rosy to be true have only to bring the image of the mental climate at the beginning of this century before their eye. Could anyone believe then that in a few decades man would land on the moon and make plans for traveling to other planets in space?

Nature will always have surprises for the intellect. Every human being—the poor and the rich alike—can be the recipients of this Grace. In fact, everyone is ordained, sooner or later, to make himself eligible for this Heavenly Boon. It is the culminating point of human evolution, and the Trophy is designed to compensate for all the effort and the agony of the climb. After that, a much more evolved, happier man will live on the earth, perfectly at home both in the inner and the outer worlds. Science and religion will have to work together to make this dream come true.

Cosmic Consciousness, being the Crown of biological evolution, must be possible with a healthy, natural life led in accordance with both spiritual and physical laws. All basic urges and survival instincts must remain intact till the end.

Unhealthy suppression of natural urges and appetites, on the one hand, and their immoderate indulgence, on the other, can only result in abnormality. In such a state the reserve of energy essential for the transformation of the brain is used up to repair, as far as possible, the damage done by excess on either side.

The basic urges and instincts of the animal still persist in man. They will continue to persist in the future man also, only in a more refined and moderate form. Extreme austerity, penance, self-denial and self-mortification are man's own creation and have no sanction from nature. Procreation is essential for the continuance and evolution of mankind. Otherwise, how can a more evolved humanity come into existence at all?

Total suppression of the reproductive urge means extinction of the race. It is only in exceptional cases, where the desire is partly or wholly absent, as a sign of highly accelerated evolution in a born mystic or genius, that it can be considered to be a natural state in such an individual. Otherwise, a healthy normal life, lived in congenial surroundings, devoted to lofty ideals and noble pursuits, ruled by temperance, truth, uprightness, contentment, compassion, tolerance, passion for self-perfection, love of the Divine, altruism and thirst for self-knowledge is the life, par excellence, for rapid evolution. This is the reason why in every gospel of faith the ideal of a good life and the cultivation of cardinal virtues are repeatedly emphasized.

Moderation and temperance are essential for accelerated healthy evolution. Immoderate passion, ambition, lust and desire, also unrestrained anger, envy, malice and hate are inimical, as they keep the mind in a constant state of unrest and turmoil. In this way, they cause disruption in the microscopic levels of the brain, where the evolutionary forces are at work, day and night, to upgrade the personality to a higher state of cognition. How can constant distraction and the remodeling of the extremely delicate tissues of the brain go on together?

We know what havoc a sudden shock, extreme grief, anxiety, pain, anguish and even anger can cause to the body. Why? Because in such agitated states of the mind there occurs a storm in the brain and enormous amounts of precious psychic energy are consumed to remedy the adverse effects on the extremely sensitive neuronic seedbed of feeling and thought. This is what Revelation came to warn against thousands of years before the birth of science.

Uncurbed lust for power, unrestricted ambition and greed are frowned upon by faith, as they disrupt or arrest the evolutionary growth. The over-clever, over-selfish and over-active brain, madly running after purely temporal ends, pays the penalty by surrendering the Immortal Crown of Illumination for the perishable trinkets of the earth. In this way, the self-seeker overreaches himself to fall prey to self-deception and self-defeat. The Laws of Heaven operate in a way that the mortal himself rewards, punishes, absolves or convicts himself.

Love, romance, adventure, sport, athletics, recreation and travel—in moderate and healthy forms—stimulate the brain and invigorate the body. Enduring love of wife, husband, children, parents, family, friends; concern for fellow human beings, chivalry, idealism, high regard for duty, truth, right judgment, forbearance, resignation, detachment and humility are the signs of healthy inner growth. Beauty, charm, melody, rapture, harmony, lovely landscapes, gorgeous scenes, awe-evoking, grand spectacles of nature, inspiring works of art, enchanting sights, sublime thoughts, moments of utter peace, prayerful moods, bubbling joy, transporting lights and pleasant odors are all, in truth, distant samples of the Supreme Experience. They all combined provide a faint foretaste of the entrancing Vision.

That which elevates, ennobles and inspires helps the Soul. Aesthetics, idealism, humanity and love are the doorway to mystical experience. All that is beautiful, harmonious, noble, blissful, true or sublime is but a warming Ray from Cosmic Consciousness. This is the reason for the use of flowers, music, incense and lights in worship and the love, longing, sentiments, hopes and aspirations expressed in prayer. Man has instinctively held to the Path leading to Transcendental Consciousness. Only his doubting reason, cupidity, lust for power and the untamed animal in him have been the cause of his frequent digressions from the Path. The vicissitudes of history represent but nature's process to teach the intellect and tame the brute. Our future generations will know better and obey the Law.

Chapter 9

Self-Knowledge
The Crown of Human Life

The crown of self-knowledge is for the saint and sinner alike. The latter, too can win it when he corrects himself and directs his efforts to that noble end. There is full hope and ample chance for everyone. The experiments done, once the biological aspect of evolution is confirmed, will gradually reveal what methods and disciplines or modes of life and behavior are suited to the constitution of each individual member of the race.

But there will always remain areas in this sublime quest of man where only Revelation can guide. Spiritual laws ruling mankind are liberal and elastic. This is evidenced by the inherent urge in noble animals for progressively more lenient and humane laws. Where the urge is suppressed or denied, Nature, in her own way, intervenes to correct the fault.

There is no reason for anyone to despair, even if complete self-mastery has not been achieved. Nature is generous and forgiving in applying the laws of evolution to human beings, as their weaknesses are well known to her. The hypocrite who poses as a saint, while still vulnerable to sin at heart, only deceives himself. Heaven condones lapses and overlooks faults, allowing full margin for the frailties of flesh and the failings in human nature.

I am myself a product of the Clemency. Divine forces meet one halfway in the attempt to uplift oneself. Why the earth has been and still is an arena of bloody struggle, sorrow, suffering and pain the investigations done by the Illuminati of the future will progressively reveal. There must be transcendental reasons for it, for the Theater of Life is the whole universe.

Who knows whence the Actors come to play their parts on the earth and what is the Plot of nature for the Terrestrial Drama of Life. There must be a consistent explanation for everything. Our brain has to evolve further and our Vision to grow broader to unravel the deeper mysteries of creation step by step.

Our earthly existence, divided into days and nights, might be symbolic of our eternal cycle of birth and death. Every night in sleep we may well be repeating the endless drama of our embodied lives when, in our dream personality, we lose track of our true identity and cease to remember that we are dreaming. Every day in wakefulness we symbolize the return of our native state of Cosmic Consciousness.

Our dreams of which some are happy, some commonplace, some romantic, some mixed, some fear-ridden, some anxious and some frightful might well be emblematic of our infinitely varied planetary lives. In this sense, the life of each one of us might be a miniature replica of the Cosmic Drama in which we act through eternity. Man is said to be a microcosm of the universe because the Eternal Actor in him repeats again and again the Cosmic Cycle in his incarnate Life.

Human life in itself is not a dream. It is a stern reality. But it is dream-like compared to Illuminated Consciousness, when the mortal wakes up to his true identity. That is why *Vedanta* compares our earthly existence to a dream or to a mirage mistaken for reality. From this viewpoint our mortal life, spent on any planet, is only a realistic dream, and our birth and death the beginning and ending of this sleep. We know not, but it might well be that we are the scattered beams of an Almighty and Unbounded Consciousness Sun whose mere thought is the universe or droplets of an Infinite Ocean whose mere act of Will has brought this stupendous creation into existence. Our own mystery is the greatest mystery of all.

Every mystical experience is a testament of our eternal life. Not the life we spend in the embodied state but a life so glorious that it ravishes our mortal senses and the mind. A life so transporting and sublime that the beholder of the vision may even swoon in ecstasy. It might be possible to understand this impact better with the help of the following illustrations:

Imagine a man in the grip of a horror dream, finding himself lost in a wilderness with haunting shadows and creeping horrors on every side. In this state of extreme suspense and anxiety, he suddenly sees a terrible lion, with bared fangs, rushing madly to devour him. He screams in terror, with his heart beating wildly and his body drenched in sweat. In that moment of utter despair, he suddenly awakes to find himself lying on his bed with cheering sunlight streaming into his room. What words can describe the relief and joy he feels at the realization that it was all a dream?

This experience, which most of us have had in varied forms, one time or the other, can convey a dim idea of the relief, happiness and wonder felt on one's first encounter with the soul. "O, Almighty God," one is led to say, "Is this the Glorious World to which I really belong? Is this living Splendor, this beaming Sun of Life, beyond this slightest touch of earthly sorrow, suffering or pain, my real Self ? O wonder of wonders, am I this immortal Being, happy beyond measure, the eternal participant in the drama of existence, sleeping and waking, like the rising and setting of the glorious sun?"

Read the narratives of great mystics born in different parts of the world and you will find ample corroboration for what I say. The regret is that we have not understood mystical experience in this right color. On the other hand, we are confusing it with visionary states and the so-called out-of-body experiences that do not bear any relation to true mystical vision that has a consistent history of thousands of years behind it in the spiritual literature of mankind.

Compare what I assert with these lines of the famous mystic of Kashmir, known as Mother Lalla:

> It is we who existed before and exist in the times to come. It is we who roamed (the universe) in the ages past and gone. The Divine in us shall never cease to take birth and die, as the sun will never cease to rise and set.

Man is ordained to know himself. Any mode of life in any environment, created by him through his own ignorance of the Law, which stands in the way of his progress on the Path of Self-knowledge, will be brushed aside by nature, as a flood sweeps aside any obstruction standing in its way. The revolutions that have occurred in the past, in the social, political or spiritual life of mankind, all bear witness to this important truth. No power can stand against or resist these cataclysms. It is only when the Law is discovered that the social, political and spiritual revolutions, necessary to conform to the demands of evolution, will be effected by the leading minds of the race without violence or bloodshed. Just as the knowledge of germs, at the back of certain virulent diseases, enabled scientists to control or eliminate the epidemics they caused, before which they were helpless in the past, in the same way, knowledge of spiritual forces will make it possible for the same scientists to control or eliminate the threat of bloody uprisings and wars before which they are helpless now. But in order to achieve this purpose the scientist will have to be illuminated also, with ample knowledge of both the inner and outer worlds.

We are at this moment virtually a witness to the Dawn of a New Age. Millions of people, all over the earth, sense subconsciously that a change is coming, but how it would be brought about and what will be the state of mankind after, it is anybody's guess. Nature has many ways to achieve her purpose. What method she would use at this time she knows the best. The change is coming because mankind has risen one more decisive step in the scale of evolution.

Some of our outstanding intellects are measuring the distant galaxies, others examining the millions of years old past record of the earth, still others exploring the depths of the ocean or the possibility of life on other planets, but only a few concern themselves with or can prefigure the shape of events to come.

The evolutionary leap taken by mankind, during recent times, is the prelude to the birth of a superior race. It will not be a new species, unrelated to us, or an invading host from another planet in space. It will be we, incarnated in our progeny, for mysterious are the ways of the soul. It is we who will give birth to nurture and rear up the new race, and it is the Divine Splendor in us that will be the participant in or the spectator of the dramas that will unfold on earth in the ages ahead. Our globe is the cradle of the Man-to-Come who, when sufficiently grown up in the body, mind and soul, will people other planets in the solar system to fulfill the Law.

There is a glorious future for humanity. Every soul has the possibility to awaken to its majesty as a sleeper awakens from a dream. We feel amazed at the marvels of technology, forgetting the fact that all this rich kingdom of science is but a small sample of the glorious kingdom of our soul, which has built it for its own edification. The marvels we have created should serve as a reminders to us of the wonders still hidden in our self.

It is the experience of Oneness in the mystical vision which shows that the triumph of one soul is the triumph of all. In the same way, the failure of pain of another soul, too, is the failure or pain of us all. It is this bond of identity among the members of the race, like the bond of unity existing in the billions of cells in our body, which alone can raise mankind to the glorious summit of spiritual illumination ordained for it.

There are clear hints about this transformation in all the religious scriptures of mankind. Only the language or the symbology used is different. All enlightened prophets, mystic and sages provide unmistakable examples of this transmutation. We, too, are on the way to it. It is this Vision of its own sovereignty that provides the greatest inspiration and incentive towards perfection to every human soul.

Excessive occupation with only worldly objective adds strength to the already powerful chains that bind it to the earth. On account of a mistaken philosophy of life, we ourselves act to tighten these chains while the aim of nature is to set us free. This is the reason for the critical conditions of the world today. Mankind is now passing through the throes of a rebirth to live a more peaceful, more happy and more fulfilling life in harmony with the Laws of God.

May Grace descend to make the transition easy and safe. May good counsels prevail to avert the threat of calamity and war. May plenty, peace and harmony increase in sufficient measure to remove want, poverty and suffering as also envy, malice and hate. And may Light Divine illumine all the minds and soften all the hearts to build a Heaven of Love, Hope, Freedom and Happiness on the earth to allow every human soul to regain its kingdom and its Glory as an immortal spark of Divinity.

Wallacks Point   Gopi Krishna
Connecticut, U.S.A.
November 5, 1978

Made in the USA
San Bernardino, CA
03 May 2014